Big Wheels and Little Wheels

By Annette Smith

Big wheels and little wheels
go round and round.

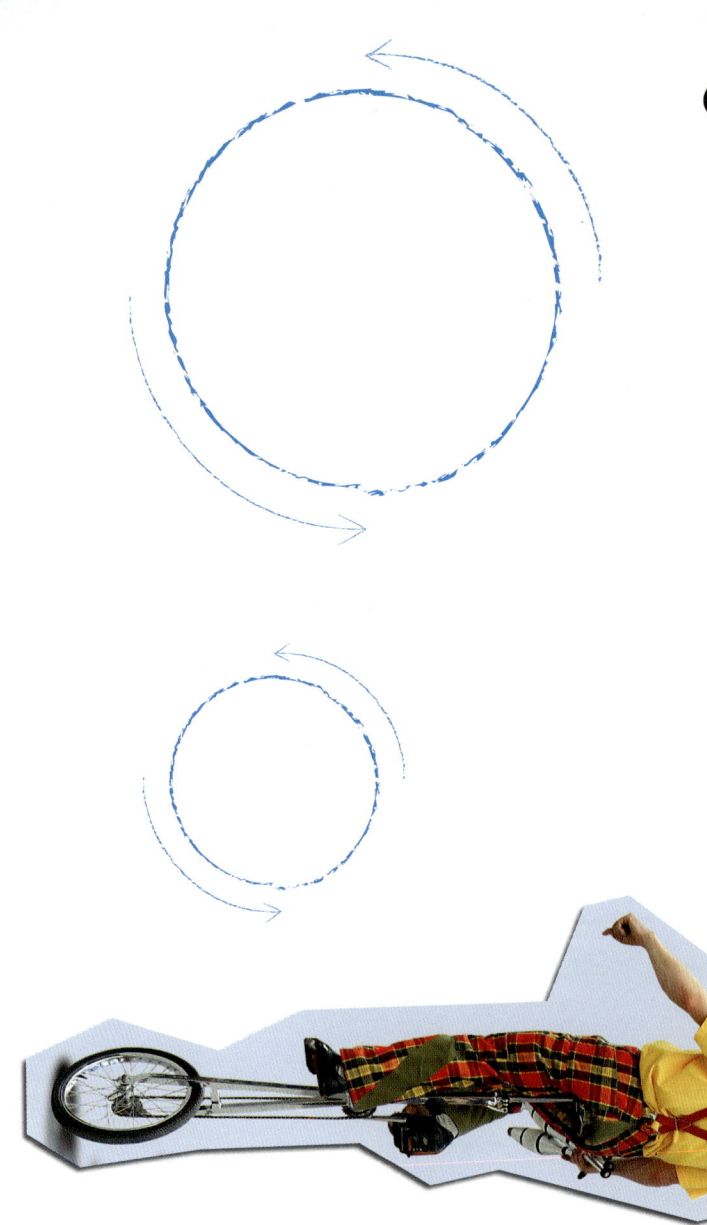

This is a big wheel.

It goes round and round.

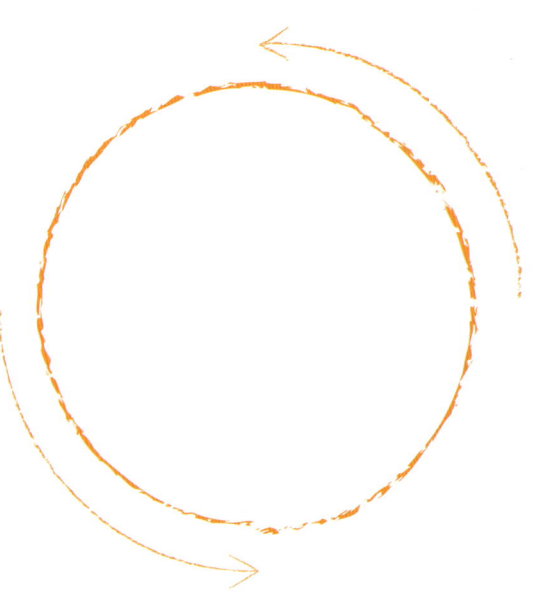

a big wheel

This is a little wheel.

It goes round and round.

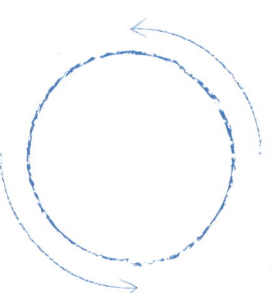

a little wheel

This bike has big wheels
and little wheels.

The wheels go round and round.

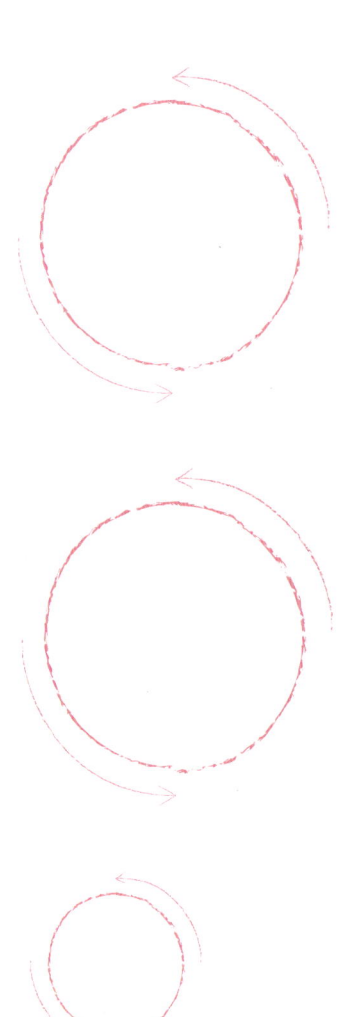

This tractor has big wheels and little wheels.

The wheels go round and round.

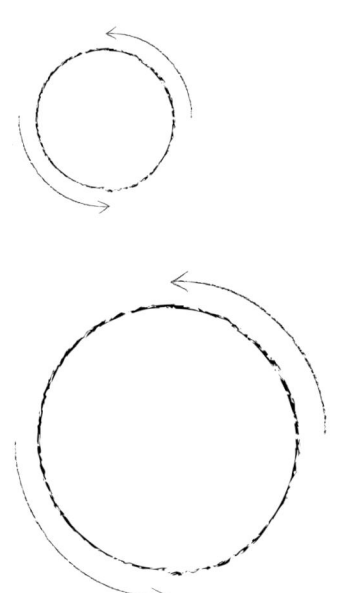

The wheels on a motor
go round and round.

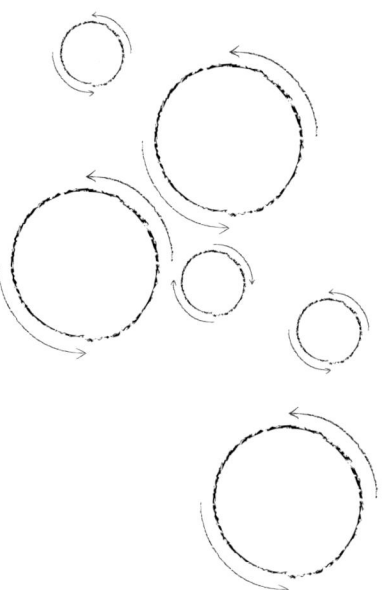

The wheels on a can-opener
go round and round.

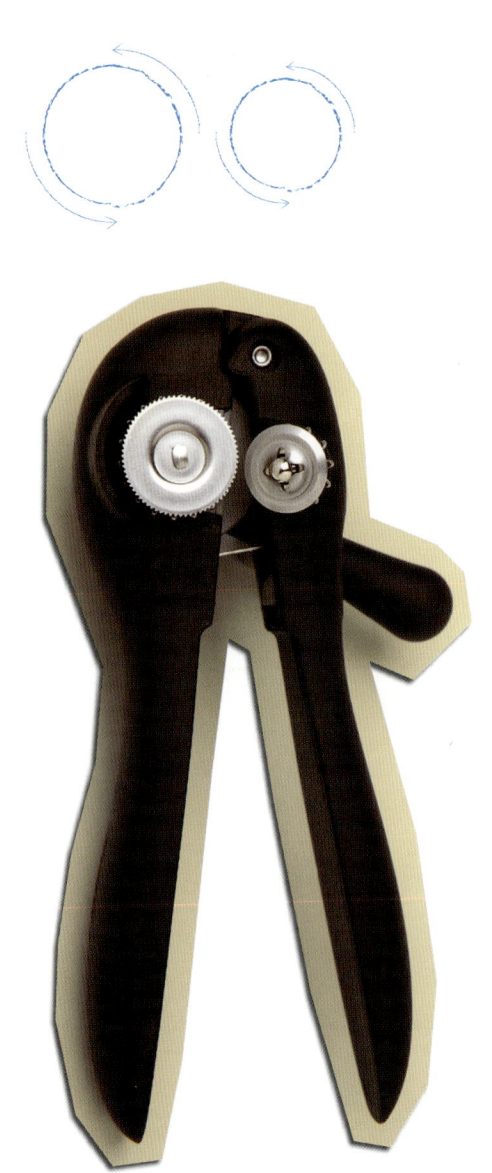

Wheels go round...

and round...

and round.